Walk Like a Philippian

Graham Baird

℘

Parson's Porch Books
www.parsonsporchbooks.com

Walk Like a Philippian
ISBN: Softcover 978-0-692-25814-9
Copyright © 2018 by Graham Baird

Dedicated to all of the wonderful
congregations that I have served
through these many ministry years.

I will always be grateful for the messages they have
each preached to me through their kindness, patience
and long-suffering love.

Contents

Acknowledgments

I am deeply appreciative of the First Presbyterian Church of Burlingame for reminding me once again that it is possible to function as a healthy church in the modern era, and at the same time be kind and caring, to all people with whom you come into contact. Thank you to my wife Star and my three children, Haley, Sheena and Ewan for their abiding faith with me through my years of ministry. Without them, I would not be the person I am today. Thank you to Lori Zimmerman for the concept for the title of this book, "Walk Like a Philippian." Lastly, thank you to the rock band, The Bangles for their inspirational song, "Walk Like an Egyptian."

Introduction

It would be hard to place a date or a time on when the first sermon in the history of the world was originally delivered. An Old Testament historian might say that the first sermon was preached by Adam himself, to his newly formed wife, Eve, after first setting eyes upon God's second human creation: "Therefore, shall a man leave his father and mother, and cleave unto his wife, and they shall be one flesh" (Genesis 2:23-24).

A New Testament scholar might cite John the Baptist as having preached the first sermon in history: "After me will come one more powerful than I, the thongs of whose sandals I am not worthy to stoop down and untie," (Mk 1:7). A theologian might put forward Elohim at the beginning of creation as having preached the first sermon, by forming the world and the universe through the utterance of a small mouthful of verbs and syllables; "And God said, 'Let there be light,' and there was light," (Gn 1:3).

An anthropologist or an evolutionary human biologist might say that the first sermon ever uttered was a hand painting etched upon the wall in the oldest-discovered cave painting in human history in Contabria, Spain, in the year 39000 BC. Contained within the essential question of when the first sermon was preached, is an understanding of what exactly a sermon consists. For some, the answer to this question is a well-articulated argument or course of action. For others, a sermon is merely an expression of one person's faith or belief system to another. In describing what a sermon consists of, perhaps it is best to paraphrase a quote from the great modern music composer Noel Gallagher, "Preaching is in the ear of the beholder."

Regardless of when the first sermon was preached, there is little doubt of two ideas. First, preaching, as a theological medium and art-form, has evolved considerably through the centuries. From the Aristotelian speaking models derived from classical Greek rhetoric that Peter and Paul employ in the book of Acts, "Fellow Jews and all of you who live in Jerusalem, let me explain this to you; listen carefully to what I say" (Ac 2:14), to the oratorically lyrical styles of the preachers of the United States in the early 1950's, "There is no rest in the heart of God until he knows that you are at rest in His grace,"[1] to the more casual teaching styles of preachers like Rick Warren at Saddleback Community Church, "God is looking for people to use, and if you can get usable, he will wear you out," preaching has moved through almost as many permutations and changes as there are different kinds of people and cultures on the face of the earth.

The second truth is that when preaching is done effectively with wisdom, knowledge, faith, healing, miracles, prophecy, and discernment (1 Cor. 12:8-10),

---

[1]Lloyd John Ogilvie, *"Do You Have Perfect Peace?"*
http:/preaching.com, (Accessed, Sept. 1, 2017).

the so-called gifts of the Spirit, it can also be transformative for the human body, mind, and soul. To this end, the modern-day Methodist preacher Will Willimon reflects on the thoughts of the reformer Martin Luther; "Where the word of God is rightly preached... demons are unleashed."[2]

With this in mind, the history of the Christian faith bears testament to the bedrock theological principle that when ordinary people are exposed to the sometimes equally ordinary words of Scripture, spoken from the mouth of an ordinary preacher, lives can be changed, new courses of action can be embarked upon, and eternal trajectories can be altered. Even self-described agnostics and existentialist Christian thinkers and theologians who generally do not believe in the actual life and historical person of Jesus, have tended to believe in the transformative power of the proclamation of the spoken Word. Bultmann, for example, writes, "Contemporary Christian *proclamation* is faced with the question whether, when it demands faith from men and women, it expects them to acknowledge this mythical world picture from the past [if so,] it would be the task of theology to demythologize the Christian proclamation."[3]

---

[2]William H. Willimon, *Undone by Easter: Keeping Preaching Fresh* (Nashville: Abingdon Press, 2009), 12.

[3] Rudolf K Bultmann, *Nues Testament und Mythologie*, English edition (Augsburg: Augsburg Fortress Publishers, 1941), 3. Italics added.

The power of preaching in my life has played an evolutionary role in my ministry. As a child, I grew up listening to my father, my grandfather, and my great-grandfather preach, all of whom were ordained Presbyterian ministers. All my homiletical progenitors served in churches in the Intermountain West of the United States and California. This West Coast preaching tradition featured a more pedestrian, rudimentary, and accessible version of the gospel of Jesus Christ, than was perhaps evident in the more formulaic and systematic forms of theology, such as those which were taught by C. Hodge, or which stemmed from eastern institutions (Princeton, Harvard, Yale, Gordon Conwell Seminary). More importantly, my preaching progenitors were heavily influenced by a strong "sovereignty of God" preaching tradition that was so prevalent among early Protestant reformers: "Truly God claims omnipotence to himself, and would have us to acknowledge it—not the vain, indolent, slumbering omnipotence which sophists feign, but vigilant, efficacious, energetic, and ever active—not an omnipotence which may only acts as a general principle of confused motion, as in ordering a stream to keep within the channel once prescribed to it, but one which is intent on individual and special movements."[4]

In my adolescent years, I was exposed to more modern voices that came from the West Coast evangelical

---

[4] John Calvin, *Institutes of the Christian Religion*, Part I (London: Bonham Norton, 1599).

preaching tradition. The most influential of these for me was the preaching of Earl Palmer, pastor of First Presbyterian Church of Berkeley, California, and University Presbyterian Church of Seattle, Washington. Palmer, as he described in an interview conducted during the Fuller Doctor of Ministry program, was influenced by many of the great preaching luminaries of his time: "John Mackay at Princeton was probably the greatest I remember. Helmut Thielicke was one of the greatest preachers I have ever heard. John Stott was a great influence. Daryl Johnson is one of the greatest living preachers. Ray Steadman. Billy Graham. It wasn't Billy's preaching, but the quality of the man that was impressive. He had integrity."[5]

Like many of Palmer's preaching influences, John Stott, Billy Graham, and Bob Munger have also been highly influential in my own life and ministry. Later, when I became ordained as a Presbyterian pastor, I discovered the preaching of more modern conversational preachers and teachers. Of this list, the most influential have been John Ortberg, Nicky Gumbel, Erwin McManus, Craig Groeschel, Andy Stanley, and Rob Bell. In each instance, the transformative impact on my life has not simply been the dissemination of information or the transmission of ideas, but the transformative power of the Holy

---

[5] Earl Palmer. 2014. Telephone interview with the author. Seattle, August 15, 2016.

Spirit to change within me not just my thinking, but my larger life's trajectory.

In my own ministry settings, preaching has played an equally transformative role. In my nearly twenty years as an ordained pastor, I have served in several different kinds of congregational settings. Most of my ministry has been in the arena of New Church Development (NCD). I have started three new churches, the most notable being Highlands Church of Paso Robles, California. In these pastoral settings, preaching has mostly served as a way of helping outsiders of the faith to become fully devoted followers of Jesus Christ. I also served as senior pastor of the First Presbyterian Church of Colorado Springs. In this setting, preaching ignited a spark of the Christian faith for people who had accepted Christ as their Savior many years before, but who now found themselves languishing in a faith system beset by boredom and intransigence. In each of these settings, preaching has been a catalyst for change in individual lives, and in the collective life of the congregation as a whole. In my current call setting, as senior pastor of the First Presbyterian Church of Burlingame, California, preaching is proving to be an essential ingredient in revitalizing an entire church system.

The late Prime Minister of Great Britain, Benjamin Disraeli, observed that "The greatest good you can do for another is not just to share your riches, but to reveal to him his own."[6] If this is true, then it must also be said that great preaching is about not just about sharing the riches found within the Christian faith, but about revealing the resources found within the hearts of individual believers and within the corpus of a local congregation. The Reformed notion of preaching (homiletics) is not simply that it is "a speech delivered before an assembled group of people," but that by some mysterious and powerful work of the Holy Spirit, it represents the voice of God to a local congregation.

This collection of messages was preached at The First Presbyterian Church of Burlingame in California in the year 2018. Perhaps more than any other lectionary-based series I have offered from the front, this message series had the impact of connecting with real people in real life challenges and situations in real time. Anyone who is reading this book, preacher or non-preacher alike, is welcome to use whatever illustrations they find in this book that are helpful for their personal situations, or their teaching life. Audio copies of these messages (CD's, or other digital versions) can be found by linking on the www.burlpres.org website or contacting the front office of the First Presbyterian Church of Burlingame.

And now, prepare your hearts and minds to...."Walk Like a Philippian...."

---

[6] *Design for Power: The Struggle for the World,* (New York: Alfred Frederick Lewis Schuman, Knopf, 1942), 200.

Learning How to Drop the Ball

It happens every year, without fail.

I have the privilege and luxury of being able to see your faces each Sunday as I look out into the congregation. I see faces that during the summer were relaxed, and happy, and calm. And every year at about this time, I look out, and I see faces that are beginning to get a little more stressed. As the fall activities pick up:

- Sports for kids
- School Activities
- Jobs in Full Swing

In short, what begins to happen is that people begin to juggle even more things than they were juggling over the summer. I talked to one young mom this past week who said to me, "Graham, I don't know how much longer I am going to be able to keep this many balls in the air." And you know? I get it.

So, this morning, I want to talk to you is how not to juggle more balls, but how to drop some of the balls that we are juggling. And more importantly, to know, to have discernment about which balls to keep going, which balls are ours to juggle, and which balls are not.

I want you to think about your life, and to think about the balls that you are juggling, and I want you to begin to think about which balls you have been juggling for a long time that aren't yours to juggle. Because God wants us to drop those.

Before I went to seminary to become a pastor, I thought that maybe God was calling me to do something else with my life. One career that I have always been fascinated by and thought for a while that I wanted to do is to be a chef. I just love cooking, and I love presenting plates, and I love making garnishes.

So, I got a summer job in college as a sous-chef in this little restaurant in Salt Lake called DB Coopers. And so, I got my whites, and my knives, and the chef said that he would teach me the ropes if I wanted to learn. And I loved it. In fact, I loved it so much, that one night the chef said, you know, this is a slow night, why don't you take over the kitchen; I'm going home. I don't expect anyone to come into the restaurant, so just close things up at midnight or so, and then I'll see you tomorrow.

So, I said great. And he was right, it was totally slow.

So, I just hung out in the kitchen. I even admired myself in the mirror because I did look good in a chef's uniform. But then, suddenly at around 10:00 a huge group of people came in from a Jazz Basketball game that just ended. I mean like 50 people. And so, I began to panic. And of course, all their orders came in at the same time. I had pans on the front burner, pans on the middle burner, and pans on the back burner. And then, at around 10:30, another group of people in tuxedos came in, around 20 people, who had just finished the symphony, and I had not even finished the first set of meals. I really began to panic. And then some of the plates that I had prepped came back because people didn't like them. By the way, never do this in a restaurant. Chef's do things to food that people complain about. I really started to panic.

Finally, the dishwasher came over to me and said, "Graham, you are only supposed to work the hot line. Do you see those other chefs over there, standing around? They are supposed to do the cold line and the deserts and the garnishes. All you must do is the three hot pans that are in front of you. That other stuff is not your responsibility.

From the children's sermon, we can also use the illustration of juggling. You know, all of us have a lot of balls to juggle.

Family Ball. All of us have the family ball. And if that was all we had to do, then we would be fine

Work Ball (School Ball) It's tough, but most of us can figure out a way to juggle work and family. Although, I did hear a fascinating study done by a recent Wharton School of Business professor that said that it is impossible to work at the top of any profession and have a family life. It is an unreasonable expectation to have for yourself.

Extra Big Project Ball. Maybe this is a house renovation, or you are building a boat, or writing a novel, or like me, a Dissertation. And you know, we can usually do that ball ok. Three balls.

X Ball (Crisis Ball, Loved One in Trouble Ball, Child Going Through Divorce Ball) Now, this fourth ball is usually the one that puts most of us over the edge.

While there are some people who can juggle four balls, I can't. There aren't many people who can juggle four balls for very long. Sooner or later, you are going to drop one of them. But what I want to begin by saying is that that fourth ball, the X Ball, is often a ball that is not our responsibility to juggle. In fact, by juggling it, we are only making matters worse.

Most of the Fourth Balls That We Juggle Are Not Our Balls to Juggle.

I was talking to a friend of mine who is a pastor who is doing a great job in his church. But every time you talk to him, he is never talking about his own church. He talks about the church he used to serve as pastor, and how badly his former church is doing. And how things are falling apart. And how he doesn't know what to do about it. And when he said this, I said, "John, that old church you used to serve as pastor is no longer your church. It's not your ball to juggle, it's not your problem.

I have told you many times about my friend and counselor, Gordie Hess, who lives here in Santa Barbara, Goleta, who I meet with once a week. He's an incredible guy. He told me the basic formula for life is this: "All human experience, and experience in conflict, can be boiled down to three questions":

Whose Problem Is It?

Most problems in life are not our problems, though we like to make them our problems. They are someone else's problem. In trying to figure out the answer to that problem, you are actually making it worse.

I sent a blog out about this not too long ago, and a woman wrote me back saying:

> Just read this week's blog re: not my problem(s). Someone on Facebook put it this way: "Not my circus, not my monkey's". Please share this with Pastor Graham. It sure fits a lot of situations that come my way.

Some problems in life are our problems. And so, those problems can be boiled down to two sub-groups. Is it a problem of values (with another person), or is a problem of resources?

A Problem of Value

Does it involve an ethical dilemma with another person, that person believes that recycling is not an important thing to do, and you do. That person feels that the only way to vote is as a Democrat, and you are a Republican, you believe that Jesus is God, they don't, or whatever...

A Problem of Resources

Does it involve that another person has something you want, or you have something that they want? In a custody battle, you want custody of the kids, and they do, too. In the sale of a home, they want the house for less money, but you want more. In Israel, it's a problem of Resources. Both groups (Israelis and Palestinians) want this small bit of land, neither will be happy until they get it.

But back to the main formula. "Whose Problem Is It?" Most of us are really stressed out about the many things we must do in this life. The many balls we have to juggle. And here's the main point of this message this morning. Many of the balls that we juggle do not belong to us to juggle. They are not our balls. They are not our problems. And if we can learn to drop the balls that do not belong to us, we can begin to live something more of the lives of shalom that God wants us to live.

Our text for the morning is one of my favorite texts and favorite books in the entire Bible. It is Paul's letter to the Philippian Church.

Paul is writing this letter at the end of his life from a prison cell in Rome. I visited that prison while I was in Rome (The Mamertine Prison). It's funny, none of the guidebooks have it listed, but it is one of the most important sights in Rome, as far as I'm concerned. As Paul was writing this letter, he was juggling many things:

- Paul's health was in decline and so he was dealing with that.

- Paul knew that he might be executed, like so many of those who line the Appian Way. Just outside of his window one could see those crucified for 100 miles.

- Paul was trying to tie up loose ends with the churches he had started, some of which were not going well.

- There were problems with Jerusalem, the Peter and James group who were trying to put stricter guidelines on who was Christian and who wasn't based on Jewish kosher laws and circumcision.

Paul was juggling many balls.

But the church in Philippi was also juggling many balls.

- They were a Roman military town about 10 miles from the coast. The Romans were always setting out on another military campaign or another and supplying troops from places like Philippi.

• Philippi was a gold mining region, and gold mining was a tough trade (as we in California used to know). It was either boom or bust. Like the stock market today, you could either win or lose a lot of money, overnight.

• There were frequent earthquakes in Philippi, which you might remember from the time when Paul and Silas were imprisoned there. The people were on edge all the time and had to rebuild regularly.

The church in Philippi was juggling many balls.

If you will, this is a text of one juggler to the other. Giving advice about how to live life, and how to figure out if a problem is actually your problem or not.

Learning what not to juggle.

This is what Paul says to the Philippian church:

Philippians 1:3-11 - *I thank my God every time I remember you.*

Isn't that a beautiful line? Remember that next Valentine's Day, or the day your wife or husband, or your boyfriend or girlfriend has a birthday. It's so beautiful.

In all my prayers for all of you, I always pray with joy.

Some have called Philippians the joy book because the word "joy" or "rejoice", or "grace" which is a derivative of the same word (*xaris*) occurs about 20 or 30 times.

Because of your partnership in the gospel from the first day until now, being confident of this, that he would began a good work in you will carry it on to completion until the day of Christ Jesus.

The idea here is so great that God will continue to improve us, make us holy, grow us, from now until the end of time. "God isn't done with us yet." Even in heaven, God will continue to bring good things into your life.

Since we are talking about dealing with our own problems and only our own problems, this is so helpful. Maybe the biggest problem of your life is always taking on other people's problems. You've always done it. You've always said "Yes" to way too many things. But that going forward, God is going to help you with that.

It is right for me to feel this way about all of you, since I have you in my heart; for whether I am in chains or defending the gospel.

Don't you feel the juggle-struggle in Paul's life here. Chains and preaching. Much of Paul's life was spent in prison, even though he needed to be out preaching and teaching. It was a great juggling game.

Paul wrote letters because he was in prison and wouldn't have been able to write if he wasn't. So, some of the struggles of our lives can produce fruit. So, in a sense, when God forced him to stop juggling (preaching, and writing), by putting him in jail for most of his ministry, he was able to only do one thing, write letters. Write.

And here's the main part for our message for today:

And this is my prayer, that your love may abound more and more in knowledge and depth of insight so that you may be able to discern what is best.

This is a bit of a mathematical equation. Like all of what Paul says:

Agape = God Love. (Paul makes up this word, there is no word for God love)

Knowledge and Depth of Insight = *Aesthesis* (esthetic)

Your Highest Love = Knowledge = Discerning What's Important

Or to put it in the language of our talk today:

Main Passion in Life = Deep Wisdom = Figuring Out What Is Your Problem

Now, I love this. What is it that drives our knowledge and depth of insight? Is it our worries? What will the stock market do tomorrow? Will I have a job? What is happening with my kids? No. Worry has nothing to do with it.

Is it our ambition? I will get to the top no matter what it takes in my job. No. It's our passion, our love which then leads to this knowing what our problem is and what isn't our problem.

How do we usually decide if a thing is our problem or not?

1. Will someone be upset with me if I do or don't do something

2. Someone else is struggling so I should struggle

3. This will impact my finances or security

4. Someone I am connected to is in trouble, so I need to be involved

Paul says, none of these should be motivating factors. The only motivation is your passion in Christ. That's it. Your highest passion in life.

And then I love that Paul doesn't leave it here, but actually tells us what is the good end product of not taking on the problems that we are not supposed to take on.

When we juggle only the balls that we are supposed to juggle, we will be *filled with the fruit of righteousness.* There will be fruits to this, and these fruits will be great, and they will be the right thing to do. And Paul continues, *that comes through Jesus Christ – to the glory and the Praise of God.* Paul is saying here that our highest passion should be Jesus Christ.

So, that's it.

1. All of us juggle a lot of balls in life

2. Many of these balls do not belong to us to juggle

3. Figuring out, "Whose problem is it?" is the beginning

4. We figure that out through our greatest passion which leads us to knowledge and depth of insight

5. When we do this, we will be filled with righteous fruit

Simple right? But it isn't simple at all for a couple of reasons.

First, because so many of the challenges of life are so murky, they are such grey areas, when someone else who is close to us is in pain, whose problem is that?

One of my favorite Christian writers is a man by the name of Frederic Buechner. Fred teaches preaching at Harvard, but really, he is a full-time writer. A great novelist and prose writer.

In one of his books, called, *Telling Secrets*, he talks about the deep pain of being the father of a daughter who is anorexic. He likens it to being trapped in a dungeon, like the tower of London. Fred talks about how in the Tower of London, which was a prison back in the day, there was a chapel right in the center of the Tower of London. But beneath that space there was this little empty room, this little tiny prison, this little room in the middle, with no rooms or no doors, just a totally dark place, called "Little Ease". And being the father of someone who is struggling with anorexia, who is killing herself by not giving herself any food, is like being in that "Little Ease" prison.

In there is a is also a small Norman chapel called the Chapel of Saint John. It is very bare and very simple. It is built of stone with twelve stone pillars and a vaulted ceiling. There is a cool, silvery light that comes in through the arched windows. Knights of the Order of the Bath used to keep all-night vigil there over their armor before being anointed by the king on his coronation day.

The chapel is very silent, very still. It is almost a thousand years old. You cannot enter it without being struck by the feeling of purity and peace it gives. If there is any such thing in the world, it is a holy place.

But that is not all there is in the White Tower. Directly below the chapel is the most terrible of all the tower's dungeons. It has a heavy oak door that locks out all light and ventilation. It measures only four feet square by four feet high so that a prisoner has no way either to stand upright in it or to lie down at full length. There is almost no air to breathe in it, almost no room to move. It is known as the Little Ease. He writes:

> I am the White Tower of course. To one degree or another all of us are. During the time of my daughter's sickness and its aftermath I began to realize how much of my time I spent in that dark, airless, crippling place where there was no ease at all. I began to understand that though in many ways we were both a lucky and loving family, my daughter's anorexia was only the most visible manifestation of a complex, subterranean malaise that we were all five of us suffering from—myself maybe most of all. The craving to be free and independent on the one hand and to be taken to the dungeon on the other hand.

I think we can all relate to some problem with which a person close to us is struggling. But Fred talks about how, giving his daughter's sickness to God, rather than carrying it himself, helped him out of the "Little Ease" prison. That in the pain of it, realizing that he really couldn't continue to juggle that ball.

Second, as Christians, one of the things we are called to do is to make other people's problems our problems, our concerns.

I will never forget an experience I had when I was living in San Antonio, Texas. Star and I were there, it was right at the beginning of our ministry, and we were trying to start a new church there called, "Wellspring." It wasn't going that well for various reasons, and I was discouraged about it. I was confused about what to do.

I went to the gym one day, which is always something I try to do, feast or famine in my life. After the work-out I went into the steam room and sitting over in the corner was one of the largest people I have seen in a while.

Then I noticed these spectacles on his face, and I realized that this was John Hagee from John Hagee ministries. And you know, it isn't every day that you get a chance to have a one on one with John Hagee. And so, I told him that I was starting a new church, and could he recommend anything in the way of that (and by the way, this is a good thing for us to remember as a new church).

He said, "the most important thing, Graham, is that anyone who comes to you with a problem, you make that problem your problem. Other people's problems are your problems." He went on to tell me that there was this woman who came to his door and needed an air conditioning system, and he bought it.

But as I have thought about John Hagee's formulation these many years later, I have to say that I may not totally agree. I think as Christians we are supposed to have other people's problems be our:

- concern
- challenge
- area of focus
- area of attention
- subject of prayer
- subject of care

But not make their problem our problem. It's called being a non-anxious presence in the therapy world.

Jesus is probably the best example of this. Though Jesus was extremely caring and loving and compassionate when people came to him, he did not make their problems his problems. He would heal people until sunset, and then feed them by the thousands, but there was also always a distance between them and Jesus. Jesus was focused almost entirely on the cross, and getting there, and nothing would stop him.

So, it's not easy. But let me offer three things that I think can help us with this, thing of not juggling every ball that comes our way, of knowing what problems ours are and what problems aren't.

First, figuring out what your passion is will put everything else in perspective.

During this strange political season in which it seems like once again, our country goes into this time of name calling and political fights, there was one story this past week that shouldn't have escaped our attention. Now, I should say at the outset that we are an apolitical church, we are a church that doesn't take sides politically. Former President Jimmy Carter announced last week that he has brain cancer. And in the way that he announced it, he was so calm and collected and at peace. He said that he might die soon. When he was asked about it and he said, "I am perfectly at ease with whatever comes. I do have a deep religious faith, which I'm very grateful for."

I used to be a Campus Minister, which is one of the reasons I am so excited about the huge number of college students and young adults that we have coming to Mission Street. There was something I noticed early on with the guys in the college ministry program. I did not notice it so much with girls. But guys would sort of serious with a girl, but not sure if they wanted to marry her, maybe sort of non-committal, until one thing happened. When they figured out what they wanted to do with their life, when they were on the main path of what they really had passion about, then they would get engaged. It was almost to a tee that some guy would tell me that he had figured out what he was going to do with his life, and then the next week, he and his girlfriend would get engaged.

And for Christians, the main passion the main thing is Jesus Christ.

John Calvin said that the main thing in life is this, "to know and enjoy God forever".

The Apostle Paul in another letter said the most important thing is love: Let love be your guide. Christ loved us and offered his life for us as a sacrifice that pleases God (Ephesians 5:2).

Karl Barth, when asked once at a symposium on theology to lay out the most important thing in all of theological thinking. He paused, and he said, "Jesus loves me this I know, for the Bible tells me so, Little ones to Him belong, they are weak, but he is strong."

Charles Spurgeon put it this way, the distinguishing mark of a Christian is her confidence in the love of Christ, and the yielding of her affections to Christ in return.

Jim Cymbala in his book, *Fresh Wind, Fresh Fire,* put it this way,

If our churches don't pray, and if people don't have an appetite for God, what does it matter how many are attending the services? How would can impress God? Can you imagine the angels saying, "Oh your worship band! We can't believe how great they are! Oh, your bulletin is so well laid out and perfect! Oh, your table outside the church where you have coffee, it is so well decorated! Oh, up here in heaven, we've been talking about it for years. I don't think so! If we don't want to experience God's closeness here on earth, why would we want to go to heaven anyway? He is the center of everything there. If we don't enjoy being in his presence here and now, why would we want to go to heaven?

So, when we figure out our main passion, it just puts in perspective all of the other things that

Second, hold other people's problems lightly.

I have a friend who is a lifeguard at a local swimming pool. It's a pool that has over 100 kids in it at a time. So, it's a hard job. I asked my friend what the key to helping people who are drowning is.

He said that the most important thing is when a person is in trouble, you have to watch them and wait for a few seconds before you dive into the pool to help them. Wait back. It will seem like a cruel thing to do, but it is the only way you can actually save them. If you go up to a drowning person when they are full of energy, they will fight you and fight you and fight you, and most often, they will actually drag you down under the water with them.

If you wait back, and just take a moment, their struggles will dissipate, and you can go in and save them.

I went to a Christian conference not too long ago in London, the Alpha International Conference with Nicky Gumble. And one of the speakers said something that I have never forgotten. She said, "If someone is crying, one of the worst things you can do is to offer them a Kleenex."

People need to grieve. People need to release. Crying is the body's natural reaction to crisis or pain. When you give someone a Kleenex you are subconsciously telling them (cover it up, stop doing that). You won't find any Kleenexes in my office.

Third, having Christ in our lives has a way of bundling our many balls that we juggle together.

Ultimately, it's Christ that is in charge of all things. Our family Ball goes in the Christ bag. Our work ball goes in the Christ bag. Our extra big thing ball goes in the Christ bag. Our extra crisis ball goes in the Christ bag.

In fact, put a lot more balls in the Christ bag, the child that doesn't talk to you anymore, the health crisis that you have having. And then, all you have to do is to juggle one bag. And anyone can do that.

Failing Forward

This morning, I want to talk about the fact that not only does God, and God only, knows what is best for us, but what God does for us, is turn our

- defeats into victories,
- our scars into stars (as Schuller once said)
- our failures into futures,
- turns our set-backs into set-forwards.

God's plan for our lives is this irrevocable, irrepressible, unshakeable movement forward. God's sovereignty in the world and in our lives is like this giant huge powerful river that moves forward through time. And so, the title of my message this morning is, "Failing Forward".

I want to ask you to think about some aspect of your life that you would define as a failure. Maybe it is something that happened in your business life, or your family life, or your marriage, or your parenting ability, or your youth or childhood, that you have been holding onto for many years. It probably won't be hard for you to summon up a perceived failure in your life, we all have them, and most of us think about those things more than any other thing we think about.

I want to introduce you to a hero of mine. He isn't a hero because he is a great success. He isn't a hero because he will go down in the record books as the most famous person to have ever lived. By most people's definitions, he is a total failure. To be specific, he has failed, many, many, many times. His name is Maxcy Filer, and he holds the record for the number of times he has failed the California Bar Exam. To be specific he failed the California Bar Exam 47 times. In an article about him in the *New York Times* it said,

> It happens with the frequency and regularity of the equinoxes. Every year, twice a year, year in and year out, Maxcy Filer takes the California bar examination. Every year, twice a year, he fails it. Every year, twice a year, his wife, Blondell, has filled out the form for the next go-round, and he'd begin studying again.
>
> Along the way, Mr. Filer has taken every bar review course on either side of the San Andreas Fault, dropping $50,000 in fees. He has journeyed around California like Father Junipero Serra, taking tests in San Francisco, Glendale, Oakland, Riverside, Carson, Los Angeles and San Diego. Someone approached his son once to say he'd taken the bar exam with his father. That was no big deal, the younger Mr. Filer replied, anyone who'd taken it in the last 25 years could make the same claim.

Filer has been taking the California bar exam since 1966. At last notice, Filer holds the Guinness Book of World Records for the number of times he has taken and failed the California Bar Exam. Let's put Maxcel

Filer's story on hold for a minute and reflect on the larger theme of failure for a moment. But let me ask you for a moment, whether Maxcy is a failure or a success?

As a person who has never took the Bar Exam, but who applied for Law School myself, and sat for the LSAT's, I can relate to the difficulty of law exams in particular, and California law exams more specifically.

But more than that, I can relate to Mr. Filer, and I bet you can too in this sense of striving for things that do not come about. Working for things that never happen. Of facing set-backs in our everyday lives.

I have faced it many times in my ministry:

> • Whether it was the once in a lifetime snowfall that hit our big outreach event in the month October, in San Antonio Texas, many years ago, that we were hosting outside in a huge park for a New Church Development event. It had literally never happened before, a snowfall in San Antonio, Texas on that date. God and I exchanged some four-letter words on that day, and I'm not referring to the word LOVE.

> • Or it was the Dad's Day Barbecue that we hosted in Paso Robles that we invited the News Media to come to. The good news was that the news media showed up, like four television stations. The bad news was that the men didn't. So, there were like 3

men there. One was my brother, who was another pastor at the church, the other was myself, the other was a wonderful 84-year-old guy named Dave Orr, who basically went to everything. He would have shown up for an afternoon of watching paint dry.

A couple of weeks ago, I was working on the Braveheart Men's Retreat. I knew how important healthy men are to a healthy church, and so I really worked hard on it. And so, I started my preparation about a month before. Carefully collecting illustrations, ideas, concepts, text, quotes. It was one of those research days where I had like four or five computer windows open at once on my computer. I had worked about four hours, and then I went to save it. And I had many documents that were called, Braveheart Men's Retreat open on my computer. So, I hit save…and you know what's coming. Judging from the nerves and the laughter in the congregation right now, you have had similar things happen to you in your life. And the computer asked me if I wanted to Replace the existing Braveheart Document with the new one. There were two documents with the same name. The new one had nothing written on it, the old one had 4 hours of work on it. I pushed yes. Four hours of work disappeared in an instant. And now you know why I was balancing on a tree limb in the forest for the men's retreat; I was short on material.

We can all relate to this sense that all that we have worked for, all that we put our time and effort into, is for naught.

That's really what the ministry of Paul looked like in many ways. If you were to look at Paul's ministry, many would define it not so differently than the life of Macxel Filer. It was one failure after another.

Ironically, his life might have been determined to be a much greater success before he became a Christian. Had he not become a Christian, he might have been a bigger success. He was a straight A student, on an upwardly mobile track. He might have been a "Pharisee of Pharisees" as he described himself once, or a "Sadducee of Sadducees". He might have been hired by Herod himself, or even the Emperor of Rome, Tiberius himself.

But then, on that fateful road to Damascus, he encountered Jesus Christ, and the rest as they say is history, and his ministry had successes, but it had, by the world's definition, many more failures. He:

> Was put in prison over and over
> Was flogged an uncounted number of times
> Faced death over and over
> Received 39 lashes from the Jews 5 times
> Was beaten with rods 3 times
> Was stoned one time
> Was shipwrecked 3 times
> Spent a day and night in the sea

Was in continual danger from rivers and robbers
Was weary and in pain often, without sleep
Was often hungry and thirsty, cold and naked
Most of the churches he started just broke into
squabbles as soon as he left.

Even as Paul writes this letter to the Philippian church, Paul's life might be considered a failure. He is in the Mamertine Prison in Rome. Paul is under house arrest.

It was probably about 62 AD, ten years after his visit to Philippi. If Paul would have been able to look out of his prison window, if his shackles had allowed him to, he might have been able to see the great Appian Way (the freeway, the I-5 of the day) where Nero had lined the freeway for 100 miles with crosses. At that point not Christians on crosses, mostly criminals. But Nero was very anti-Christian. The historian Tacitus tells us that when the great fire burned Rome on July 18, 64 AD, that Nero blamed the Christians for starting it.

It was not looking good for Paul or for Christianity.

And yet, it is from this place of failure that Paul writes these words. These words of hope, and love and joy:

Philippians 1:12-26

Now, I want you to know, brothers and sisters, that what has happened to me has actually served to advance the gospel.

And by "happened to me" at this point, Paul is talking about all the stuff we just talked about. That the things that would normally slow down, or impede the future of, or prohibit success, have made it so that the gospel has become more successful.

Now, two things to note here.

First, this idea that "what doesn't kill you makes you stronger" (a quote that is attributed to Nietzsche) was totally foreign to the thinking of the time. The Roman world was all about muscular strength. The Gladiators were events which tested who was strongest, and only the strongest man lived. It was an early form of survival of the fittest, of social Darwinism. The weaker person always died. And death was always seen as failure.

But this theology, which is of course at the heart of Jesus' ministry, but which is propelled by Paul, "My grace is sufficient for you, for my power is made perfect in weakness." Therefore, I will boast all the more gladly about my weaknesses, so that Christ's power may rest on me. (2 Corinthians 12:9) begins to permeate the entire Christian way of thinking. It's counter-intuitive. It's paradoxical.

And it's even a step further than the proto-typical faith of the Jewish people. For 2,000 years before the Jewish people had believed, had deeply believed that when you are in peril, when you are in trouble, when you experience hardships, God will and can intervene and bring you out of those hardships. That's what the story of Joseph in Joseph's Technicolored Dream Coat are about.

The story of Joseph is how God found him in prison in Egypt and brought him out of prison and helped him rise up to lead the Egyptian Empire.

But what Paul is saying is even more bold than that. Paul is saying that that thing in your life, which you perceive as a failure, that thing is a success in and of itself. Without even being saved out of that failure, there is success within the failure for the gospel. Paul is saying that sometimes God brings us out of the wilderness into the promised land, sometimes, but that always, the wilderness can be a place of success.

It reminds me of when I was growing up. My mom is Scottish, and she always used to tell us that what is bad luck for everyone else is actually good luck for you, because you are Scottish. She used to say,

- Black cats, bad luck for others, good luck for you.
- Walking under ladders, bad luck for others, good luck for you
- Spilling salt, bad luck for others, good luck for you
- Friday 13th? Bad luck for others, good luck for you.

So, on Friday 13th if we saw a black cat and spilled salt and walked under a ladder, we would all go out as a family and buy a lottery ticket. Our friends thought we were crazy. That impression that some others have of the Baird family hasn't changed over the years.

Second, notice that Paul doesn't say what has happened to him has actually served to advance him. No, it was the gospel that was advanced through Paul's failings, and failures.

As a result, it has become clear throughout the whole palace guard and to everyone else that I am in chains for Christ. And because of my chains, most of the brothers and sisters have become confident in the Lord and dare all the more to proclaim the gospel without fear.

And then, Paul begins to opine about all of the religious hucksters there were around him, with which many of us can relate. There are a lot of good churches out there, of all different denominations and creeds, but there are also a lot of bad ones, or I should say, churches that just don't get it, and often produce bad ends.

It is true that some preach Christ out of envy and rivalry, but others out of goodwill. The latter do so out of love, knowing that I am put here for the defense of the gospel. The former preaches Christ out of selfish ambition, not sincerely, supposing that they can stir up trouble while I am in chains.

There were some Christians at the time who were actually happy that Paul was in prison. They thought he was a trouble maker. A rabble rouser. A renegade.

There were Christians who were praying that Paul would stay in prison, or even better be beheaded (which eventually happened a few years after the writing of this letter).

Paul's response is – what does it matter. There is a very famous and very important Jewish phrase for this, are you ready for it? (Ee ahhh….). Paul says EAAHHH.

The important thing is that in every way, whether from false motives or true, Christ is preached. And because of that I rejoice. Yes, I will continue to rejoice, for I know that through your prayers and God's provision of the Spirit of Jesus Christ what has happened to me will turn out for deliverance. I eagerly expect and hope that I will in no way be ashamed but will have sufficient courage so that now as always Christ will be exalted in my body.

And here is the most radical thing he says about this "Failing Forward" stuff…*whether by life or death.* Even in death there is success for God. And Paul here is not just talking about the fact that he will be resurrected from the dead because he believes in Christ for eternity, but the death itself will move the gospel forward.

Now it's important to note that this death, which Paul lifts up, is not self-imposed, or immolation, or self-destructive death. No, but the natural death that comes to all of us, the death that sometimes the world puts us through.

For to me, to live is Christ and to die is gain. Paul is saying that death itself is gain. *If I am to go on living in the body, this will mean fruitful labor for me. Yet, what shall I choose? I do not know.*

There's a part of Paul that would rather die. He's sort of had enough of this life. Which, by the way, my 99-year-old grandma can relate with. She told me the other day, I am just ready to die. I've had a good life. I am ready to start my next adventure.

I do not know. I am torn between the two, I desire to depart and be with Christ, which is better by far; but it is more necessary for you that I remain in the body (that I not die). Convinced of this, I know that I will remain, and I will continue with all of you for your progress and joy in the faith., so that through my being with you again, your boasting in Christ Jesus will abound because of me.

It's the most radical and powerful and hopeful account of the gospel that, outside of the lips of Jesus, has ever been written by another human being. That not only will God bring you out of the pit, as the book of Psalms writes, on occasion, but that the pit itself is success for the gospel. And that when we are in the pit, we can know that God is doing good things in that space. Maybe better things than God might be able to do if our lives were "successful" by worldly standards.

So, this is the second sermon in our Philippians series. And I'm so excited to be looking at this book together over the next month or two. For me, it is my favorite book in the New Testament. Because it is so hopeful, and it is so full of joy, and it is so full of life. And mostly I love it because it conveys this sense of God that God is all powerful, and that God will carry forward whatever God wants to do, no matter what happens in the world. That God's love, God's plan is like a giant river, that flows forward, until the end of time.

I went to a college in the Midwest called Macalester College. It's in St. Paul, Minnesota. I went on a bagpipe scholarship, which is a story for another day! But growing up in the Intermountain West, I had seen many huge mountains. But I had never seen huge rivers. I had backpacked in the Sawtooth's, the Whiteclouds, the Rockies, the Tetons. But I had never seen a great river. And so, when looked upon the great Mississippi River for the first time, I was dumbstruck. I had never seen a river so large, or so powerful, or so mighty.

I had seen lakes in Idaho that were smaller than this great river. But the river was not a stagnant body of water. It moved with huge force and might. Now, the Mississippi River does not move with speed, it moves with might. It is a slow-moving water. And I remember thinking, where does this river begin, it must begin from a huge Glacier in the north in Canada or something. But someone said, no, the headwaters of the Mississippi River is in Northern Minnesota, and it begins as a tiny trickle out of the ground. I couldn't believe it. So, one summer, I drove up to Northern Minnesota, and sure enough, there was the headwaters of the Mississippi River, a tiny trickle.

And that as the river moves forward, it picks up more water as it grows, but here's the thing I learned. As the river goes, the river also picks up logs, and rocks and silt, and debris. In some parts of the country, the river will pick up couches and chairs and old refrigerators, and just carries those things all the way down to the Gulf of Mexico. The power of the river is not just the water, it's the debris!

The water is God's sovereign power in the world. God's plan for the universe. God's plan for our lives. The debris, the rocks, the trees, the couches, those are the failures of our lives. And what God does, is he doesn't kick those failures out of our lives, he doesn't throw them out of the river, he carries them along with the river, and makes the river stronger, more powerful, more mighty.

Now, that's easy to say, and it's a nice image, but failure hurts, it doesn't feel good, it isn't pleasant. So, I have three ideas for you.

First, when hardship is hitting your life, holiness is hitting someone else's life.

In my 20 years of ministry, I have seen this in spades. To the point where when I am going through hard times, I almost get excited because I know that good things are happening to others all around me.

- When I have had the biggest session/church arguments, the most baptisms were happening in the church.

- When people have left the church over a dispute, God has always brought even more people after that.

- When I am getting critiqued the most, someone somewhere is noticing how many things I am doing well.

- When I feel that weight, that I can only describe as spiritual weight on my shoulders at times. It is not really depression, it is just a spiritual weight, I know that somewhere, somehow God is doing great things. And I rejoice.

It has gotten to the point where I almost look forward to the hard times because I know that through them, God is doing something great somewhere else.

C.S. Lewis took this theology to a new level. He talked about transpositional healing. When his wife Joy got cancer, he prayed to God every day that God would move the cancer from Joy on to himself, so that he would die and that his wife would live and would not be in pain.

Second, God always interrupts our hard-times or failures with reminders that he is still looking out for us.

Not too long ago, I had to make a hospital visit on someone early in the morning. Now, the only similarity I share with my great predecessor pastor of this church, Tom Gillespie (Gillespie was way out of my league in so many ways), but the only similarity is that he was not a morning person, and I am not either. So, it was early in the morning. Like 5:30, and I had to make a hospital visit. The only harder thing about waking up early and doing a hospital visit is that the person I went to visit was not available to meet with me when I got there. So, it was a waste. I had a huge day in front of me. I am sitting in the lobby, it is like 6:30AM. The vacuum cleaner guy is going through the waiting room because there is no body in the hospital at this time. There is a woman sitting next to me. I strike up a conversation with her. I ask he why she is there. She tells me that she is there to wait for her father who is in surgery. I give her my business card and tell her I am here to help you if you need anything, I'm a pastor just down the street. She looks at the last card and says, "Your name is Baird? My family name is Baird. My dad is Scottish, a Presbyterian. Do you know anything about Scottish Presbyterians?" I'm like, I know a thing or two. In my hardship that morning, God was right there with a reminder that he was still looking out for me.

Now, I don't know what God was doing for Paul as he was sitting in that prison cell at the end of his life. I don't know if maybe one of the guards was giving him some good food to eat, or a nice wine. Or he was just in this inexplicable happy place that only God could explain. But Philippians is a book that sounds like a guy who is so happy, he is high on drugs. Joy, Joy, Joy, Joy, Grace, Gratitude…. But I guarantee you this. As Paul was suffering in prison, God was sending him some reminder that He was still looking out for Paul.

Third, Christianity is a faith that has suffered more failures and setbacks, and always become stronger because of it.

Andy Stanley recently preached a sermon in which he talked about going on a tour of Rome, seeing the Colosseum where the Gladiators fought. And he reached one little door, archway, where there was a cross over the doorway. And Andy asked the tour guide what that was. The guide said it was a doorway for the Christians to enter before they were killed.

Stanley says reflected on the fact that at the time, it would have seemed that Christianity was doomed. But that by some miracle of God, Christianity, as it was being stamped out, was succeeding more than it had ever done. And from this Andy says this for all of us. Remember these things:

1. Remember, in your most discouraging moment, there is a cross hanging over the Emperor's Gate in the Roman Coliseum.

2. Remember, People are going to name their kids Paul and Peter. They are going to name their dogs Nero and Caesar.

3. Remember, one day there will be no Roman Empire, but the church of your Savior will be in every nation in the world.

4. Remember, you will do profitable things with your life, but you will never do something more significant with your life than build Jesus's church because it is the activity of God on this earth.

It's what it means to Fail Forward as a person of faith. That in that dark moment, God is doing something bigger than you could ever imagine.

Oh, and one more thing. Not long ago, Maxcey Filer died.

He died in 2001 at the age of 80. But not before he passed the California Bar Exam. Before he died, Maxcey Filer took the California Bar exam one more time. A few months later, the results of his exam came back in the mail. He didn't want to open it because he had received rejection so many times before. He had failed so many times before.

His son, Anthony, a guy who had passed the bar exam himself, years before, did the honors. Maxcey Filer, the dad just went to the living room to watch "Matlock". "I heard all this commotion," said Filer the dad, "Daddy passed the bar! Daddy passed the bar! I stood there, looked at some champagne, and said, I'm not going to drink it, I'm high enough, I don't need anything else." At the age of 61 he finally passed the bar exam!

But why are we talking about Maxcey today? Is it because he passed the bar exam? No. Thousands of people do that every year. We are talking about him, because through his failures, God did something great. And God can do the same through you too!

Harmunity: The Harmony of Unity

Last week we offered kind of counter-intuitive message about how sometimes God turns our scars into stars, sometimes God turns our defeats into victories, sometimes God turns our setbacks into set-forwards, sometimes God takes us out of the wilderness and puts us in the promised land, but that always God uses our failures and our hardships to do big things for the kingdom.

We like to think that God can only really use us when we are "successful", but that Paul, who is in prison as he is writing this letter, is reminding us that God can use our failures sometimes even more than our successes.

God's plan for our lives, for all of creation is like one giant river, that flows forward, and that that river is part of God's power of the river is the water, but part of the power of God's power are the boulders and rocks and trees and couches and fridges that float down that river, and those objects are made a part of God's great river.

I told you that one of my recent personal failures was that while working on the men's retreat, I didn't save the right document on my computer, and lost like 10-15 hours of work. Which reminded me of a true-life argument that happened recently…

So, the Devil and Jesus were having an argument one day, not too long ago about who was the best computer programmer (this is definitely a joke for Silicon Valley). And they were going back and forth and back and forth. Which was the best computer programmer. "I am" said Jesus, "No I am" said the Devil. "I AM" said Jesus", "No I Am" said the Devil." "I Am I Am" said Jesus, and so it went on and on.

And then God from up on high in the heavens, who couldn't take their arguing anymore said, "ENNOUUUUUUGH!" And at that moment, the whole universe disappeared into darkness. When the lights came back on again, there was Jesus and the Devil sitting in front of their computers. And so, God said, "alright, whoever designs the best computer program in the next 20 minutes wins.

And so, the Devil and Jesus went at it again, clicking, coding, clicking coding, and then the universe went dark again one more time. The universe lights went back on again, and both computers were sitting there. Both totally blank. The Devil tried again to get everything he had lost. But nothing worked. Jesus pushed one button on his computer, and instantly everything came back up on his screen. No way, said the Devil, how did you do that? Jesus looked at the Devil in the eye and said – "Two words…Jesus Saves!" (I told you that was a joke for Silicon Valley).

Okay, that joke, strangely enough is what I want to talk about today.

• I want to talk about the chaos that disunity, that argumentation, that fighting, and bickering can bring to the world. And I want to talk about the peace, the happiness, the joy, the harmony that can come from when people come together in unity.

• I want to talk about the feeling that all parents get, who, like God, want to yell at the top of our lungs, EEENOOUGH! Because bickering between kids is so tiring to be around.

• And for no one is that possibly more true than for mothers. For moms, when your kids are getting along, when they are sharing happily, when they are happily playing with one another, or if you have older kids, if your kids just really love one another. And almost nothing can bring a mother's heart more angst than when there is disunity or cacophony.

I mean, we really prayed about one gift that we could, as a church, give to all moms here today. Some person said, "We could buy all moms here a giant box of chocolates." But you know, would that really be a gift to moms? It would be when they were being eaten…but a little later on…. "Thanks, Burlpres!"

And we thought of other things, like free trips to Hawaii. But you know, a free trip to Hawaii, can still set you back about $10,000…cause nothing's free in Hawaii.

And so, we really prayed about it. And we realized that what we could give moms that would mean the most would be to reflect for a moment or two upon this notion that when things come together, when your kids are getting along, there is peace. There is Harmony. There is Harmony in Unity. There is Harmony in Unity. There is Harmony in Unity. In fact, I have even come up with a new word for it, which is the title of my message this morning....

HARMUNITY

Harmunity is the Harmony of Unity! We want to give all moms here today, and all moms watching on Facebook the gift of – Harmunity! And the Harmony of Unity can only come from one thing and that is Humility. And that's what we are going to talk about today.

So, way back in the day, before Star and I had young kids, we used to go to movies together. And one of the things I loved most about going to a movie, was not necessarily the movie itself. But the part that I would always look forward to was that incredible THX sound snippet in the beginning of the movie. The sound clip goes from this place of total cacophony, of all these sounds bouncing off one another, and not harmonizing with one another, but then, slowly but surely, all the sounds come together to one single sound.

Now, because we do not actually have THX sound in our chapel/sanctuary (although that would be cool, and if someone in the church wants to spring for a new THX sound system for the church that would be fine…) we can't get the real effect of this. But even from our own sound system, you can feel how jarring the cacophony is, and how pleasing the unity is.

And no-one gets this better than parents. I mean, you can find yourself in the most aesthetically pleasing place in the world:

• You can find yourself in a four-star restaurant being served Cordon Bleu cuisine, but if your kids are bickering, there is no joy in that moment. You would rather go to McDonalds and eat a happy meal by yourself, than to be in that restaurant at that moment.

• You can have a nice long day of a day off, but if there is argumentation in the house, it is really vexing. You'd almost rather be at work. The book of Proverbs says this, "It is better to live on the corner of the roof, than to be in a house with a quarrelsome person." (Prov. 21:9)

• Your kids can be going to the best schools on earth, the best teachers, the best everything, but if they are not getting along with other kids in the school, or the other kids are not being nice to them, you would almost rather just keep them home from school altogether.

• You can be on vacation in the most pristine, beautiful, gorgeous place on earth, but if your kids are arguing, or not getting along, you can sometimes wish that you weren't on vacation at all.

During my first summer vacation after my freshman year of college, I was working in an oil refinery to try to help pay for my tuition. But because my younger siblings, my brother and my sister were not yet in college, and because mom and dad thought it would be nice for them to go on vacation one last time, for one last vacation before the kids left home, and they went to college, my mom and dad and brother and sister all went to Scotland. Now, Scotland, as you know is one of our favorite places on earth.

There is literally no place on earth that my family would rather be on vacation than Scotland. But for whatever reason, and we can probably chalk it up to adolescent angst, and post-pubescent development, my brother and sister were arguing the whole time. And I wasn't there, so I don't know exactly what happened (because I am the older brother, and older brothers are always out working in the fields, when younger siblings are out squandering their family inheritance...no I'm not bitter) but apparently the story goes that Dad got up to the Highlands somewhere, somewhere between Kyle of Loch Alsh and Inverness, when my father, not being able to take it anymore, literally turned the car around in the middle of the road, and started to drive back to the airport in Edinburgh to call the whole trip off.

Disunity, argumentation, disputation, bickering, dispute, fighting can be so awful to be around, that it just wears on our souls. And what is always the case is that the fighting is always bad for the two people who are involved in the fight, but it is actually often worse for the people around the fight who have to experience it.

• It's bad for North Korea to be picking a fight with the rest of the world, but it is worse for Japan and South Korea that have to be near it.

• It's bad for the country of Israel and Palestine to be in a fight, but it's almost worse for surrounding countries (Jordan, Egypt) to be near it.

• It's bad for a couple who are married (or divorced) to be in constant argument with one another, but it's worse for the kids who have to be near it.

And now, this is a very simple sermon, because the remedy for all argument, all dispute,

All bickering is one thing. It is HUMILITY. If we were to write out an equation for this on the board it would be:

Harmony + Unity = Humility

H + U = HUM

or the opposite is also true

Cacophony + Disunity = Angst

C + D = A

• Humility comes from the Latin word HUMUS – which literally means ground, dirt, earth. The notion is that humility is literally lowering yourself to the ground. Which as Christians we know that we were made of earth, or ground, Adam was made of earth, or ground, and so it's a remembering of who we really are.

• It's also where we get the word humiliate, which literally means to put someone else down to the ground, to put them to the earth.

• The Greek prefix for lay down or put yourself down in front of is *pros*. *Prospito* means to prostrate yourself before. *Proseuchemai* means to pray. A funny thing about this is at relates to Paul is that Paul is in prison. And yet he prays all the time. He would often be shackled to a guard who is next to him. But that didn't stop Paul from praying on his knees. And so, when Paul went to his knees to pray, so did the prison guard. (I guess it was a new form of prison evangelism).

And the reason that humility works to bring about unity is because humility is a natural emotional boundary that people have with one another. If a fight is caused by assertion on both sides, then the best way to figure out how to lower the temperature is if both people create an emotional or spiritual boundary.

The best example of this is driving a car in Burlingame, California. I just love living in Burlingame, but it took me a little while to get used to the narrow neighborhood streets.

Because the streets of Burlingame are so narrow in places, there is only room for one car to pass. And so, to drive here regularly, you must get used to what I call the "Burlingame Wave". And the Burlingame Wave is that when another car is coming your way, you often pull to the side where there is an opening in cars, so the other car can get through. To let the other car, know you are doing that, you give them…" The Burlingame Wave" (that's two fingers just over your steering wheel). And then they pass, and then, they in turn, return the…. "Burlingame Wave". The only way to drive here successfully, is for everyone to know that you have to let cars through occasionally. You have to defer to the other cars. You have to lower yourself, humble yourself to other cars, to let them through. If you don't or if both cars don't, you just get jammed in the middle of the street.

Now a quick point before we move to our text for mothers who have bickering kids. But children are often developmentally incapable of that kind of self-lowering, by their very nature, they are self-focused, their first word is often "No" and their second word is "Mine." And so, that's why boundaries are important.

Where you find households where there is a lot of conflict, 9 times out of 10 it is caused by bad boundaries. There are boundary problems between:

- Both parents (parents are arguing, and this causes conflicts with kids)

- Parents and children (not respecting space, not allowing flourishing souls, too protective)

- Spatial boundary problems (literally all in one space)

Ok, let's talk about our text. Paul is nearing the end of his life, he knows it. He senses intuitively that the Roman Empire has finally caught up to him, he is in prison, he is likely to die, part of him wants to die. His body is falling apart. He has broken bones from the times he has been beaten, that never really healed properly. He's got a lot of things not going well, however, one of the most vexing, frustrating things that Paul must deal with are these ongoing church fights which have taken root in almost every one of the churches he started.

And one of those churches that is causing Paul not to have HARMUNITY in his soul is this little church in Philippi.

Philippians 2:1-11

Therefore, if you have any encouragement from being united with

Christ. There's our word unity, and notice, one of the keys to unity with one another is being united with Christ.

If any comfort from his love, if any common sharing in the Spirit, if any tenderness and compassion. This series of "conditional if's" in a row is a classic Greek rhetorical tool. You see this in old English too, Shakespeare used it all the time (in Hamlet), *"To die, to sleep, sleep, IF perchance to dream"*

Then make my joy complete by being likeminded, having the same love, being one in spirit and of one mind. Paul is directly addressing what we are talking about this morning. Like mindedness, same love, being one in spirit, one mind are the recipes of joy, or as we are calling it *harmunity.*

Now, behind the scenes of this wonderful letter that Paul is writing to the church in Philippi is argument that is going on. And we will never know what kind of argument that was, but Paul refers to it, obliquely again and again. In fact, he addresses it head on at the end of the chapter; "I plead with Euodia and Syntyche to be of the same mind in the Lord. Yes, and I ask you, my true companion, to help these women since they have contended at my side in the cause so he gospel…" (Phil. 4:2-3). This church argument is deeply vexing to Paul. Literally, on Paul's death bed, he is asking them to stop bickering.

And by the way, if you have ever been in a church where there was a church squabble, there is almost nothing worse. A friend of mine told me about a church conflict once where the elders were so up in each other's business, and arguing, that after the elder meeting one night, one of them went out to the church parking lot and slashed the tire of another elder. Issues…

Do nothing out of selfish ambition or vain conceit. Don't just assert yourselves all the time. You gotta give people the "BURLINGAME WAVE" and let them pass on by.

Rather in humility – which by the way, is a different word than *prospipto*, but it is particularly important for Mother's Day, because here Paul uses a feminine word for humility, *tapeinophronsyne*. Paul seems to be saying there is something uniquely feminine about the kind of humility that is required to create unity.

Value others above yourselves, not looking to your own interests but each of you to the interests of others.

And then, Paul does an amazing thing, he uses an old church hymn sung in the early church, in order to compare the kind of humility that we need to have as humans to Jesus' humility to become human, to live our lives, to die on the cross. Let me just read this whole section as one unit, and not comment on it as I go:

In your relationships with one another, have the same mindset as Christ Jesus, "Who, being in very nature

God, did not consider equality with God something to be used as his own advantage; rather he made himself nothing (lowered himself to the ground), by taking the very nature of a servant, being made in human likeness. And being found in appearance as a man, he humbled himself by becoming obedient to death, even death on a cross.

And because Jesus did this, God lifts Jesus up to the highest place, and because Jesus is lifted up, we then must lower ourselves on bended knee to Jesus, and then Jesus will lift us up too.

This idea of humility is so hard for us, I think hard especially for Westerners, and perhaps mostly Americans, who sometimes just have a hard time with this idea that there is more strength in bowing down to another person than there is in self-assertion. But it is something that the Eastern world, particularly the Asian world can help us with.

So, this morning, on Mother's Day, my own mother in law and father in law are here visiting us. They live in Tucson, but they are here for a week. And I will forever be grateful to my parent's in law, not only because they raised the most amazing woman I've ever met, my wife Star, and they gave me permission to marry her (and yes, I did ask permission, I am old fashioned), but they gave me a deep love and appreciation of Asian culture. My father in law is an Asian law professor, has taught all around the world, Harvard, Vanderbilt, Tokyo, Washington University, University of Washington.

And so, when Star and I got married, John and Karin started to give us some original paintings by an amazing Japanese Christian artist named, Sadao Watanabe. He lived from 1913 to 1996. And what is amazing about Watanabe, is that his painting was a form of humility and faith in and of itself. Here is an article that was printed about him before he died:

Sadao Watanabe was proud to be known as an artist-craftsman who used a centuries-old technique of textile dyeing to create contemporary art prints. With his glasses permanently perched on the bridge of his nose, he would kneel on tatami matting by a work table in a small studio in his Tokyo home and begin the laborious process of creating stencils, which served as the key blocks for his unique style of graphic art.

Watanabe would literally bow down on his knees to pray and to paint. Here is a picture of Watanabe on his knees in his studio:

Here is a painting of Noah's ark. Notice that even the animals themselves have a sense of humility about them.

Here is Jesus washing the feet of his disciples. Notice not only Jesus bowing down to the disciple, but the disciple bowing down to Jesus

Here is the Watanabe that is hanging in my office. Notice the angels and their bowing down to Jacob, and Jacob bowing down to them.

A devout Christian, he viewed himself simply as a channel through which the power of God worked and believed that "profound faith will inevitably assume the form of profound beauty." Every new print sheet was, in the words of his biographer Masao Takenaka, "a fresh discovery of beauty given by grace."

So, thanks to John and Karin, Star and I own around 10 of Watanabe's original prints. And so, I have been looking at them and studying them for about 20 years now, as Star and I have been married for about that same time. And one unique quality that all of the prints have, which are all based on Biblical scenes, is that they all have this incredible HUMILITY to them. They all have the main characters literally bowing down to one another or to God.

Here is a painting of Jesus being taken off the cross, notice the bowing down of the disciples as this is done,

Here is Mary and Joseph on the road to Bethlehem, notice Joseph bowing down as he is walking in humility

Here is Jesus washing the feet of his disciples. Notice not only Jesus bowing down to the disciple, but the disciple bowing down to Jesus

Here is Jesus picking up a little lost sheep, notice Jesus bowing down to the sheep

Here is the Watanabe that is hanging in my office, please feel free to come by and look at in any time. It is of the upper room, and the disciples who are praying there, notice them bowing down to the Holy Spirit

And one has to say, on this Mother's Day, that there is something distinctly feminine about these depictions of humility.

Humility = Harmony and Unity

So, that's it, it's a simple message. But one last thing.

First, only when Jesus enters our lives is true harmunity possible.

I have so enjoyed the Joseph's Amazing Technicolored Dream Coat Productions that our Church has put on.

And I have been deeply honored that they also asked me to come and play bagpipes during these performances as a kind of gag intermission performance. And whenever I play the bagpipes, people always ask me how they work. What is the instrument exactly? And I always tell people that it is not just one instrument. It is four instruments. It is three drones, in the background, that's what goes (uuuuuuuu), and then there is the chanter, which is the fourth instrument (that's what goes, da, da, da, da, da da da). So, it is really a hard instrument, because you are really playing four instruments at once.

But here's one thing that every piper will tell you. If you ever find an occasion where all four of the instruments in a bagpipe are in perfect harmony, which is a trick, and almost a miracle. There's the old joke, "How can you tell if a bagpipe is out of tune, someone is blowing into it". But on rare occasions, when all of the drones and the chanter are in perfect tune, when they are in perfect harmony, when they are in perfect unity, then this mysterious thing happens. A fifth instrument can be heard. A mysterious fifth instrument arrives in the mix.

I can tell you, in my 23 years of playing bagpipes, it has only ever happened to me once or twice. Once was when I was playing for a wedding at a great beautiful Catholic church in Manhattan for a wedding. I was playing, and all of a sudden, there it was, the fifth instrument. It was like goose bumps on the arm.

Jesus is that fifth instrument in our lives. He is the mysterious instrument that comes into the mix, when the other instruments are in perfect harmony, perfect unity That's when something truly holy happens...

The Power of Words

I began two weeks ago with a message about how God sometimes uses our failures and our hardships even more than he uses our successes to advance the kingdom of God. That sometimes God turns our Scars into Stars, that sometimes God turns our Defeats into our Victories, that sometimes God turns our setbacks into set-forwards, but that always God uses our wildernesses, our failures to bring about the kingdom. We compared God's sovereign plan for the kingdom being this great river that flows inextricably forward. That our failures are like those logs and trees and couches and fridges that are in the river, that God envelopes and pulls us forward.

Last week, on Mother's Day, we talked about this gift that God offers to all of us, this notion of a Harmonious Unity, or Harmunity as we called it which is only possible through two means, that is through our focus on Christ, and Christ's servanthood, and on our own attempts to be humble to seek humility. And humility is not thinking less of ourselves, it is thinking of ourselves less. It is taking our whole being (the good stuff and the bad stuff) and bowing down before one another. It's giving one another Burlingame Wave, as we allow others to pass. And that this is particularly difficult for children to do because they are concrete thinkers and their frontal lobes are not fully developed, so boundaries are so important when trying to find harmunity within our homes.

This morning, what I want to talk about is, ironically, talking. This morning the word that I have for you is the power of these things that are coming out of my mouth right now, our words.

Today is Pentecost Sunday. That means that 1,985 years ago, the CHURCH as we know it, was born. It began in an upper room, as we saw from the children's sermon, where the disciples were in prayer. As far as we know, these prayers were silent prayers. But then, a Holy Wind comes into the room, tongues of fire emerge, the disciples leave the upper room and go out into the streets. And by some miracle, they start to SPEAK, in languages that they had not known before.

Now there were staying in Jerusalem God fearing Jews from every nation under heaven. When they heard this SOUND, a crowd came together in bewilderment, because each one heard their own LANGUAGE being spoken. Utterly amazed the asked, "Aren't all those who are SPEAKING Galileans? Then how is it that each of us hears them in our own native LANGUAGE. Parthians, Medes, Elamites, residents of Mesopotamia, Judea, Cappadocia, Pontus…. we hear them declaring the wonders of God in our own TONGUES.

There is no other way of saying it. The church began, the church was created through WORDS, through SPEECH.

That when God created us in his image, when he created us male and female, he gave us this incredible power, the power to speak, and with these utterances that come out of our mouths, we have the power to create, or to destroy, to build-up or tear down, to give praise or to give rebuke. And that at this juncture in our American life together, we need to pay more attention to – The Power of Words. But first, would you pray with me?

One of the things I love most about the part of the world that we live in are the huge number of incredible museums that we have right here in the Bay Area. There are so many great ones. A short list includes the:

- Legion of Honor
- Exploratorium
- De Young Museum
- San Francisco Museum of Modern Art

And a zillion others. Perhaps to try to keep up with San Francisco, I recently heard about a new museum that is going up in our Nation's Capital, Washington, DC, that is entirely devoted to Language. The NML, or the National Language Museum. NML's mission is to, "inspire an appreciation for the magic and the beauty of language." Ironic that this museum is being formed in a place where language, on both sides of the isle is less than inspiring. Among some of the more amusing exhibits are an entire section devoted to mixed metaphors or mixed idioms. Here are some of my favorites:

"Don't judge a book before it's hatched"

"Every cloud has a silver spoon in its mouth"

"It's not rocket surgery"

"You can't teach a leopard new spots"

"We'll burn that bridge when we come to it"

And my all-time favorite, "You've opened your can of worms, now lie in it"

Now these are funny, for several reasons, the first is because, in a way, we all know that words come from a place of reality in our brains, that we think, and then we speak. So, reality starts here (in our brains), and then we speak what comes out. The realities of our lives are formed even before we speak.

We are all now familiar with the new tech devices like Alexa or like Siri that we ask a question, and then the computer gives us an answer. "Siri, what's the chief end of man?" Siri, "The chief end of man is to glorify God, and to endure him forever." A recent scary but fascinating scientific example of this is a new computer program that is being perfected at a thing called the Media Labs at MIT, where brain waves into reality, even before we speak them. Scott Pelley, of 60 minutes recently had a fascinating interview with a young scientist about this new technology. Here is the interview:

Arnav Kapur: What happens is when you're reading or when you're talking to yourself, your brain transmits electrical signals to your vocal cords. You can actually pick these signals up and you can get certain clues as to what the person intends to speak.

Scott Pelley: So, the brain is sending an electrical signal for a word that you would normally speak but your device is intercepting that signal?

Arnav Kapur: It is

Scott Pelley: So instead of speaking the word, your device is sending it into a computer.

Arnav Kapur: That's correct.

Scott Pelley: That's unbelievable. Let's see how this works.

So, we tried him.

Scott Pelley: What is 45,689 divided by 67?

Arnav Kapur: Sure.

He silently asks the computer and then hears the answer through vibrations transmitted through his skull and into his inner ear.

Arnav Kapur: Six eight one point nine two five.

Exactly right.

Arnav's research seems to bring new meaning to the most famous sermon that Jesus preaches, the Sermon on the Mount. Jesus said that the sins of our lives actually occur before they are committed. They begin in the mind or the heart. So, if we think about killing our brother, we have already done that thing in our minds. "If you call your brother a RACA, with your words, you have already murdered him." If we think about committing adultery, we have already done that thing in our minds.

So reality begins here, and then it is transmitted into WORDS

But then, these mixed idioms or metaphors are funny, because in a way, when we speak the reality that comes from our brains, and then words are formed, we also create reality with those words. That these utterances that come out of our mouths are not just verbs, and subjects, and objects and conjunctions, they are vehicles of creation all around us.

Nowhere is this more apparent than in the way that the Bible tells us that the world was created. God literally created the world by speaking.

In the beginning God created the heavens and the earth. Now the earth was formless and empty, darkness was over the surface of the deep, and the Spirit of God was hovering over the waters.

* *And God SPOKE (said) – "Let there be light, and there was light".*

* *And God SPOKE (said) - "Let there be a vault between the waters to separate water from water. And there was sky"*

* *And God SPOKE (said) – "Let the water teem with living creatures, and let birds fly above the earth, across the vault of the sky, so there were creatures"*

It is WORDS from God that bring about creation. And we see this extended all throughout the Bible, wherever God SPEAKS, there is creation.

Even where humans speak there is creation.

As if to prove the power of words in the midst of creation, when early humans are on the face of the earth, after the time of Noah and the flood, the book of Genesis says that (Gen. 11:1), *"The whole world had one language and a common speech."* They began to form cities and nations with their common speech. And one day with their common speech, they said, *"Come let us build ourselves a city, with a tower that reaches to the heavens, so that we may make a name for ourselves."* And they began to build in fervor. And they were actually quite successful by all accounts. And God, for whatever reason, mostly for fear of their own avarice and greed, decides to slow this group of humans down, by confusing…what? Their SPEECH. *The Lord said, "if as one people speaking the same language they have begun to do this, then nothing they plan will be impossible for them.* Notice the close connection of speech, and possibly HARMUNITY we talked about last week. So, what does God do? He confused their WORDS. *"Come let us go down and confuse their language so they will not understand each other."* And with the confusing of language. And of course, that city was named BABEL, and the word BABEL would forever be associated with confusing speech, confusing words, with words that make no sense.

To this day, when preachers like me begin to wander, congregants all say, "What is that preacher babbling about?"

Jesus enacts a series of miracles in the New Testament, through nothing more than the power of WORDS.

- Jesus's first miracles in the Gospel of Luke, A man with an impure spirit, Jesus comes up to him SPEAKS, "Be Quiet, Come out of him." And he is well.

- Jesus heals Peter's mother in law, he leans over and SPEAKS, and "rebukes the fever." – bad fever, get out, and it leaves.

- A man with Leprosy wants to be made well, Jesus Speaks, "Be clean" and he is made well.

Every one of Jesus' miracles occurs because of mere WORDS. Sometimes the words are accompanied by laying on of hands, or spittle, or washing, but there are always WORDS.

And what we believe as Chris followers is that all of us are made in God's Image. That

God put a little bit of himself in all of us when he created us. And one of the things that sets us as humans apart from other creatures is the gift of language. Sure, perhaps whales can communicate through songs, and monkeys through gestures, and even song birds through songs, but no other living thing that we know of, has this power of SPEECH the way we as humans do. And just as speech is a creative force for God, so it is a creative force for humans.

If you notice a bit more lightness or giddiness in my step this morning, that may be because just this past week, I learned that after 7 years of hard work, I finally finished my Doctoral program. My project was approved, with distinction (incredibly). Please don't call me Dr. though, though that is what I am making my kids do. "Daddy, can we have a play date?" "You mean Dr. Baird; can we have a play date?" But I will tell you in my seven years of completing this degree in Theology, one of the most important things I learned is that Theology is not some arcane set of rules or guidelines, or esoteric formulas. No, Theology is a two-part word and it is simply meaning, GOD SPEAKS, **Theo-Logoi**, God speaks!

So, speech, words, language are an intrinsic part of creation, and of our creative ability as humans. But, just as WORDS can be a constructive, creative force in our lives, and in the world, so can they also be a destructive force. These utterances that come out of our mouths can tear down, they can stop us from being what God wants us to be.

• It is speech, words, from the lips of a snake that leads to the Fall of Adam and Eve. It is not the eating of an apple the causes the Fall, or even the lying about it later. Those would contribute to the Fall. But the Fall of humanity begins with a simple set of words from a snake in a garden, "SSSSS…. That tree won't hurt you, SSSS…. That fruit isn't bad to eat."

• It is grumbling speech, words, from the lips of the Israelites, who while in the wilderness for 40 years, overcome so many tough things. They overcome the greatest army on the earth the Egyptians, they overcome the lack of food, and water, they create one of the first set of laws ever to be written. But it is their words, their GRUMBLING, which prevents them from achieving their goals.

• Just this past week, we saw yet another terrible example of the gun violence which is gripping our nation. This time, again, in a high school, where a young man took out a weapon, two weapons a shotgun and a 38-caliber pistol and killed 10 people and wounded others. This one doesn't make sense. He seemed like such a nice young man. Just three words that were found on his Facebook page on a tee-shirt, "Born to Kill". Those words seemed to have some power in this young man's life.

And it is grumbling that Paul wants to remind the church in Philippi about in his

letter to them. And it is the power of Praise that Paul is trying to remind the Philippians of through his own modeling in this week's segment of this letter.

Philippians 2:12-18

Therefore, my dear friends, as you have always obeyed – not only in my presence, but now much more in my absence – continue to work out your salvation with fear and trembling. This is picking up on what we talked about last week, the theme of humility. And it is also where Soren Kierkegaard gets the title for one of his most important books, "Fear and Trembling". What Kierkegaard and Paul mean here is not fear of God – but total HUMILITY.

For it is God who works in you to will and to act in order to fulfill his good purpose. Here's the image of the river once again, a great powerful river that moves forward, and brings about God's will, no matter what.

And here's where Paul brings up the topic of grumbling and of arguing, and its destructive impact in our lives:

Do everything without grumbling. Let me repeat that, *Do everything without grumbling.* Everything? Yes, everything. You mean, we can't grumble even when we have reason to grumble? Yes. What about...

- That <u>health problem</u> that slows us down...yes, don't grumble about that

- That <u>employee</u> who just bugs you...yes, don't grumble about that

- That <u>political situation</u> which seems impossible ... yes, don't grumble about that

- That <u>church conflict</u> that never goes away...yes, don't grumble about that

- That <u>bill</u> that you don't want to pay...yes, don't grumble about that

- Those <u>kids</u> that drive you crazy...yes, don't grumble about that.

- That <u>spouse</u> who really doesn't understand you...yes, don't grumble about that

The Greek word Paul uses here is GONGUZMOS, which is an onomatopoetic word, which is a word that sounds like what it means. GONGUZMOS, is what it sounds like when people are grumbling. It's interesting, the Hebrew word for grumbling, MURMER, is also onomatopoetic. MRMRMRMR.

But why? What's so bad about grumbling? Well, we don't know exactly why Paul tells us not to grumble, but possibly it hearkens to what we talked about at the beginning of the message. That words create reality. By grumbling about something that creates something in and of itself.

Also, Paul throughout this letter seems to embody this philosophy of not grumbling. Because if anyone has a right to grumble it's Paul. He's in prison, his life is coming to an end, his body hurts all over, his life's work is very much in question. But Paul doesn't grumble, even when he has a right to. In fact, Paul does the opposite. He uses hopeful words throughout this whole letter.

- He uses the word Rejoice at least <u>15 times</u>

- Often, he says it twice in a row. *"Rejoice, and again I say Rejoice"*

- And when he isn't using the word rejoice, he is using some other hopeful, uplifting word:

Grace, Peace, Thanks, Partnership, Unity, Affection, Best, Truth, Love, Life, Remain, Encouragement, Sharing, Glad, Cheer, Confidence, Righteousness, Prize, Crown….

This short letter is a panoply of optimism!

Do everything without grumbling or arguing, notice Paul seems to be saying that grumbling leads to arguing. *So that you may become blameless and pure.* Again, notice that it is our words which pollute us, not just our actions. *"children of God without fault in a warped and crooked generation." Then you will shine among them like stars in the sky."* Notice, all we have to do to shine, to become stars is to be careful of our WORDS.

As you hold firmly to the WORD of life. WORD of life, God's WORD. *And then I will be able to boast on the day of Christ that I did not run or labor in vain. But even as I am being poured out like a drink offering on the sacrifice,* Paul is literally saying that he is becoming like steam, *and service coming from your faith, I am glad, and REJOICE with all of you. So, you too should be glad, and REJOICE with me.*

So hopeful, so uplifting, so full of life and love.

So, this is a simple message, just two quick points to ponder this week:

First, words can destroy.

My grandmother in law was a great woman of faith. She lived, until she turned 100, and then summarily died on her 100th birthday, as if to say, "Ok, I'm done, now I'm going to heaven," in a rural cabin in the Smoky Mountains of Tennessee. She prayed all the time. When she wasn't praying she was going to church, like two or three times a week. She always used to say, "Graham, I want you to know that I pray for you every day." And she did.

But what was so remarkable about Mary Ellen was that nobody ever heard her say a negative thing about anything. She just never did it. She had a hard life, a wife of an army colonel who came back from WII with a world of issues, she never grumbled. In fact, whenever she didn't like something, she never said, "I don't like that." She would just pause and say, "Well…now, isn't that interesting." I mean, I don't care what it was that you told her, she never said anything negative, she just said, "Well…now isn't that interesting."

She was a lifelong Republican, I mean, she had a picture of George Bush on her mantel piece right in the center of her room. And if you ever went up to her and said, "Grandma, what about Hillary Clinton, don't you think she is a good Senator?" She would say, "Well…now, isn't that interesting." She loved the Braves. Watched them all the time. If you came up to her and said, "Grandma, what about the Giants, I think they are a much better team." She would say, "Well, now isn't that interesting." She's in heaven right now, looking down on me preach, and I'm not sure what she would think of this sermon, but I can tell you what she is saying watching this sermon right now, "Well…now isn't that interesting…."

And why didn't she say anything negative? Because she knew that Words can Destroy, Words can bring down, words can diminish, words can hurt.

Second, words can create, heal and save.

Just yesterday, those of us who weren't watching the Warriors play basketball, might

have turned our attention to the royal wedding of Prince Harry, and Meagan Markle. It was a stunning worship service. A Royal Wedding. Music, and Costumes, and Choirs, and Pageants, and Crowns, and Diamonds, and Regalia.

But what is a wedding really? It obviously isn't about all the costumes and music and pageantry. It is an exchange of WORDS. It is an exchange of WORDS before a bride and a groom, before a couple and God, before a couple and a congregation.

And with WORDS, with two words, I DO, and I WILL, and SO HELP ME GOD, a couple begins a holy relationship that binds them to one another.

And there were other beautiful words at that wedding. "I Harry, take you Megan to be my wife." "I Meagan, take you Harry to be my husband," "For Better or for worse, for richer or for poorer."

And other beautiful words, Stand by me, from a choir. The Power of Love, from a preacher.

And over the years they will need to learn other words, that will be just important:

- I'll Get That
- I'm On It
- Don't Worry
- Hang in There
- I'll Work on That
- I'm Sorry
- I Forgive You
- I Won't Do That Again
- I Didn't Mean to do that

And if they want to find a guide book on where to find those words, the book of Philippians wouldn't be a bad place to begin.

Rejoice Always, and again I say, Rejoice!

Can God Use Your 'B' Game?

We are on our fifth week of our series called, "Walk Like a Philippian," in which we are looking at this letter that Paul writes in about the year 62AD, as he is in the Mamertine Prison in Rome. Things are looking bleak for Paul, as Nero has occupied the throne, a crazy king and ruler, and the end of Paul's life seems imminent and near. And yet, this is the most uplifting book in the entire New Testament, and perhaps the entire Bible. It's uplifting because:

As we saw in our first week, it demonstrates this inextricable force and power of God to take all the things of our lives, the hardships and the failures, and everything in between, and like a giant river that flows forward, Paul says that God can use the failures of our lives even more than the successes. That sometimes God takes our scars and turns them into stars, but sometimes, God uses our scars for the kingdom. God always uses our failures to build up the kingdom. The kingdom of God is like this river that just moves forward, picking up all the debris of our lives (the tree limbs, the rocks, the silt, the couches) and moves it forward.

And it is uplifting because, as we saw in our second week, on Mother's Day, God gives each of us this gift of Harmunity, the Harmony of Unity. And the only thing we need for this gift of Harmunity, is humility. It is not thinking less of ourselves, but it is thinking of ourselves less. It is doing the Burlingame wave, as we pull to the side of the road and let people drive past us.

And it is uplifting, because, as we saw last week, Paul uses the most encouraging words for us and over us. Paul uses the word Rejoice at least 15 times in this letter. And in case we don't hear that word, he often repeats it twice in a row, "Rejoice, and again I say rejoice." He uses words like "Glad" again and again, and "forward", "cheer", "hopefulness", encouragement." And at the same time, he warns us against the words that we use in our lives. He warns us against grumbling. That words come from a place of reality in our hearts, and that words create reality. And as humans, as Christians, we can either create or we can destroy with our words.

This week, Paul is equally encouraging as he reminds us that not only can he use our failures, but that the things we think of as successes in our lives, are not that big of a deal. Especially for God. That the things that we consider to be our "A Game" are for God, sometimes less significant for God than what we think of as our mediocre performances. Or our B Game. So, as we prepare for our Word this morning, I want you to think about:

- The biggest honor you have ever received
- The most important award
- Or the highest distinction
- Or the biggest trophy

And then, I want you to think about perhaps something in your life that you don't consider to be a failure, exactly, but it just wasn't your best performance. Perhaps you might consider that to be your "B Game". And what I want to ask this morning is a basic question, "Can God Use Your B Game?"

So, up here on my stool this morning is a rather grandiose statue. It looks like something you might see in an art museum. But it is a trophy. I received this trophy when I was still in High School. It has been with me, and when I say, with me, I mean, I have quite literally packed it up in boxes wherever I have moved for the past, 28 years. To give you some context for that. I received this trophy when I was 18 years old, and this weekend, I am turning 46, so I have been packing this thing around with me, wherever I have moved since I was 18 years old. I have been toting this huge thing around with me, almost twice as many years, as I was old when I got it. It is a trophy for winning the National Oratory Championship when I was 18 years old. The national competition was held in the auditorium of San Jose State University, just down the road from here.

It really doesn't mean much to me anymore, it's not that big of a deal, it's no BIG THANG…and that's why I take it with me wherever I go….

Since I won this award, I have literally moved something like 12 times. So, 12 times, I have packed and unpacked this thing. Wherever I go, it comes with me. Because I have packed it and unpacked it so many times it has seen its share of wear and tear. It used to have two big handles on each side. They have been knocked off. And it used to be shinier. And the words used to be on the front, now they are on the back. It's squint.

Now, to be honest, I don't remember much about my speech, or the moment. I look back at pictures of myself at that age, and I hardly recognize myself. Really, I was just a kid.

Star has been trying to get me to throw it out for years. Because really, where do you put it? It doesn't exactly go well with much interior décor, unless you are really into a very Rococo form of Greco Roman art. You know, it doesn't really match with the rest of our IKEA furniture.

Here's the question. Why have I toted this thing around with me all these years? I guess because it represents a moment for me when I really brought my "A Game" to something. I guess it represents a time when I could say to myself, and to anyone who was listening, "Ha, I won." "I'm a winner." "I'm the best." And I guess I have told myself all these years, that if I don't bring my A Game to something, then it simply won't be good enough.

And I know if we had the time to go around the room this morning, or for those of you watching on Facebook, you too have similar honors, awards, trophies, distinctions, medals in your life. I mean, to be honest, you wouldn't be here today if you didn't. You can't really live in Burlingame, (You wouldn't be living in Burlingame, if you had too many examples in your life of bringing your B game) to reach this level of worldly success unless you had gotten your fair share of;

- <u>Degrees</u> from distinguished universities
- <u>Recognition</u> for best salesperson of the year
- <u>Top of your class</u> in law school
- Spelling Bee <u>Champion</u>
- <u>Magna</u> Cum Lauda
- <u>Teacher</u> of the year award
- PTA <u>President</u>
- <u>Lettered</u> in Multiple Sports

Unlike me, maybe you haven't been packing up your actual award with you wherever you go (or maybe you have). But maybe you have been carrying it with you in your heart.

And since I gave that speech in San Jose in 1990, I have given countless other speeches, and sermons. Many of them much less quality or in any way elevated.

One of the worst of them (one of the biggest examples of my B game) might have been a talk I gave in a nursing home not too long ago. I love speaking in nursing homes, because, you know, to be honest, they don't always have to many other options for entertainment that afternoon. It's sort of a captive audience. It's like prison ministry. And I don't know what was happening that day, but my brain wasn't really working that well. And I was making this illustration about the country of Cuba. And I was trying to talk about the former dictator of Cuba, but I couldn't come up with his name. The room was full of people who were on average, 90 years old and above. And I hesitated and said, "The dictator of Cuba was named, was named, was named…." I couldn't come up with it. Finally, a 99-year-old woman in the back raised her hand and said, "You mean, Fidel Castro?" "Yes, Castro, thank you." And you know if a 99-year-old is prompting you for a speech, you might not exactly be bringing your "A" game. At best, it is probably going to be considered your "B Game". Afterwards, on the way out the door, I could hear a group of seniors saying, "He, He, what do they teach these kids in school these days…didn't know the dictator of Cuba's name…He He." Because it is the nursing home where my grandma lives in Pasadena, I go back there regularly. And I swear, each time I go down, people remind me of that speech, where I couldn't remember the name of Fidel Castro. "Ha, how's your knowledge of world history going Graham?" "Can I buy you a Cuban Cigar?" They ask. I mean, they are still talking about that talk, that "B Game talk" to this day.

And to be honest with you, no one is still talking about my National Oratory Win "A Game Speech" except for me…

Here's my question, which speech, the one that I gave in San Jose in the year 1990, when I was 18 was more important? Or the speech I have in a nursing home. My so called "A" Game, or my "B" Game? Which speech did God use more, my "A" Game, or my "B" Game?

One of the things that I have noticed is that often the things that we consider to be our best material, our best stuff, our best effort, is not actually what others consider to be our best effort. Let me show you what I mean? I'm going to give you a list of famous people, and when I tell you their works, tell me which one you are more familiar with, or like the most?

CS Lewis

- A Preface to Paradise Lost (or)
- The Lion the Witch and the Wardrobe

Who has read A Preface to Paradise Lost? Who has read the Lion the Witch and the Wardrobe?

A Preface to *Paradise Lost* is considered one of Lewis' biggest academic contributions, and he really wrote *The Narnia Tales* as a sort of fun, don't take it too seriously hobby. In other words, Lewis's "A Game" was his "Preface to Paradise Lost". His self-described "B Game" was the Narnia tales. And yet it is his "B" game that we talk about and read to this day.

Leonardo Da Vinci

- The Virgin of the Rocks (or)
- The Mona Lisa

Who knows of *The Virgin of the Rocks*? Who has heard of the Mona Lisa? The *Virgin of the Rocks* was commissioned to fill a huge altarpiece, he spent hours and hours on it, it's attention to detail is unassailable. It was his "A" Game. Or *The Mona Lisa*. The second painting, the most famous painting in the world was commissioned on a small scale, wasn't supposed to be a big deal. Just a painting of a woman. People stand in line all day just to see this painting in the Louvre, for a minute or two.

Earnest Hemmingway

- Three Stories and Ten Poems (or)
- The Old Man and the Sea

Who has read Three Stories and Ten Poems? Who has read the Old Man and the Sea? Hemmingway spent years working on his first book, "Three Stories and Ten Poems". He poured himself into it. It was what he might have called his "A Game". The Old Man and the Sea, he wrote very quickly after he went on Safari in Africa, in 1951, almost as an afterthought. He might have said it was his "B Game". It is considered one of the greatest short stories ever written.

Stephen Curry and the Warriors

- Game two against the Rockets in which Stephan scored 16 points and lost (Or)
- Game three against the Rockets in which Stephan scored 35 points and won.

Who liked game two against the Rockets better? Who liked game three against the Rockets better? Curry said that he played much harder in game two, where less points were scored, than he scored in game three where more points were scored. In a way, Curry thought that he brought his "A" Game in game two, and his "B" game in game three. I'll take more of Stephen Curry's B Game…!

This contrast between what we view as important or significant in our lives, and what the world sees as important or significant are two different things.

But that's not really what I want to talk about this morning. What I want to talk about is…

The difference between what the world sees as important or significant, and what God sees as important. What we view as our "A Game" God often views as our "B Game". And what we view as our "B Game", God can often do much more with.

In the first century, in Jewish society, the mark of an "A Person" or an "A character" was not what part of town you lived in, or what college you got a degree from, or how many trophies like this one that you received in high school. The mark of your A Game was, simply put, how righteous you were. And how righteous you were was tied entirely up with how much you held to the "Jewish Law." This is why Jesus is always being brought to task by the religious authorities about how he has broken the law (the Sabbath codes, Cleanliness codes, The Shema, The Ten Commandments).

If you will, the trophies of the day, the National Oratory Trophies that people clung to, were their outward appearance of religious righteousness.

Again, today it is different. The mark of success for our world is not tied up in righteousness, but in outward success:

- Where we live
- What we drive
- Where we go to school
- What awards we get
- How much we make

And one of the strange marks of righteousness was whether you were circumcised or not.

And not just if you were circumcised, but which rabbi circumcised you, where it was done (what temple, what synagogue), on what day of the year, what day of the week. A person's "A Game" could be determined, if you were a man, by this strange rite of passage.

And for whatever reason, this Philippian church is totally caught up in this debate. This debate is totally dividing this church.

Philippians 3:1-14

Further, my brothers and sisters, rejoice in the Lord. As if Paul hasn't said the word rejoice enough in this letter, he is saying it once again. *It is no trouble for me to write the same things to you again, and it is a safeguard for you.* Notice, for Paul, the amount of joy we have in our lives, is synonymous to our Spiritual health.

And then, he points out this strange debate about circumcision.

Watch out for those dogs, those mutilators of the flesh. These people whose trophy, who's sign of success is this sign of righteousness (self-righteousness). And what these people were doing is making people feel bad if they weren't circumcised, and then they would oblige and help you out with that, and usually it was done with a blunt instrument, that wasn't sanitized.

For it is we who are the circumcision, we who serve God by his Spirit, who boast in Christ Jesus, and who put no confidence in the flesh. Who put no confidence in our "A Game"? Who put no confidence in our awards, no confidence in our trophies, no confidence in our degrees, no confidence in our medals, *though*, says Paul, *I myself have reasons for such confidence.*

Paul then talks about how in modern terms he the most successful person of his generation was. He was the champion.

If someone else thinks they have reasons to put confidence in the flesh (in their A Game), *then I have more. Circumcised on the eighth day, of the people of Israel, of the tribe of Benjamin* (the prized tribe, youngest son Jacob, and the younger brother of Joseph), *a Hebrew of Hebrews, in regard to the law, a Pharisee as for zeal, persecuting the church, as for righteousness, based on the law, faultless.* I was in my "A Game" says Paul. All the time.

But whatever were gains to me I now consider a loss for the sake of Christ. Whatever my trophies were, whatever my awards were, whatever degrees I got from whatever universities, I consider a loss. They are worthless.

What is more, I consider everything a loss because of the surpassing worth of knowing Christ Jesus my Lord (knowing Christ is the A Game), *for whose sake I have lost all things* (lost all my worldly awards, all my trophies).

I consider them garbage. Garbage? Garbage? Really? Those awards that he worked so hard to get? Yes, Garbage. What Paul is saying is that this trophy here, should not be on a table for all to see, it should be put in the garbage.

[Graham puts his National Oratory Trophy in the garbage]

That I may gain Christ and be found in him, not having a righteousness of my own that comes from the law, but that which is through faith in Christ – the righteousness that comes from God on the basis of faith. I want to know Christ – to know the power of his resurrection and participation in his sufferings, becoming like him in his death, and so, somehow attaining to the resurrection of the dead.

Not that I have already attained this, (this A Game that can be found in Christ), *or have already arrived at my goal, but I press on to take hold of that for which Christ Jesus took hold of me.* Paul is recognizing that he is living this B Game existence in the reach for Christ, but he is reaching, reaching for that A in Christ. *Brothers and sisters, I do not consider myself to have taken hold of it. But one thing I do. Forgetting what is behind* (forgetting all the trophies) *and straining toward what is ahead. I press on toward the goal to win the prize* (to get the A in Christ), *for which God has called me heavenward in Christ Jesus.*

It's such a powerful text about our own sense of self. How what we think is important is not what God thinks is important. How all of us are on this journey of faith, where every one of us reach for the prize in Christ, that is the Christian journey!

I don't know about you, but all of my heroes, are people who have given up the rat race of life to try to get medals and honors and trophies that the world considers important and reaches the prize in Christ.

• Eric Liddell, a Scottish minister (featured in the movie Chariots of Fire) who won a gold medal in the 1924 Olympics but gave it all up to be a missionary in China.

• Dr. James Loder, who was a PhD in the History of the Philosophy of Religion, from Harvard University in Philosophy, one of the smartest men ever to get that degree, gave up an illustrious career to teach ministers at a seminary in New Jersey – I was one of them.

• Thomas Merton, who had the best education money could buy, and was left a fortune by his parents to live comfortably on, left it all behind, and became a Trappist monk and lived and wrote at a seminary in Kentucky.

• Simon Weil, one of the most significant thinkers and people of faith of the 20th century, was born into an affluent Jewish family in Paris. She was extremely intelligent. Served as a cook for soldiers fighting in the Spanish Civil War.

And the list goes on and on. All people who left their trophies behind, their so call (A Game), and took up the (B Game of Christ), to reach for the Cross.

And I just love it when normal ordinary people say to themselves, what I have to offer isn't going to be fantastic, but I am just going to offer it anyway and see what God can do with it. My favorite example of this was one of the best sermons I have ever heard in my life. It was preached by Bob Mitchell in Colorado Springs. Bob had been a great evangelist in his life. Brought thousands of kids to Christ through Young Life. Had been President of Young Life International. I asked him to preach, he was 91 at the time. At first, I had thought it was a great idea, but then I wondered. We had to build a ramp up to the front for him to walk up. As he tottered his way to the pulpit, I had my doubts. But then Bob spoke. "My name is Bob Mitchell and it is an honor to be standing before you today. Frankly, at my age, it is a miracle to be standing at all…." And then Bob preached one of the finest sermons I had ever heard. He couldn't do it for memory anymore, he didn't have the punch he used to, but it was even better, because it was his "B Game for God".

And maybe that's you. Maybe you've been waiting around the church, don't want to get involved, because you can't give us you "A Game". Fine, give us your "B Game" we'll take it. God can do even more with that.

Just three quick thoughts for you to consider this week:

I. Our "A Game" Isn't as Good as We Think It Is.

There's kind of a funny book out now, called, "You're Not as Great as You Think You Are, A Demotivational Guide". One credit said this about the book, "This book turned me from a winner into a wiener in one sitting. It works!" Chapter titles include, "Chicken Coops for the Soul, limiting the power of your imagination," "The Power of Negative Thinking," "Giant Steps Backwards, the art of setting self-defeating goals", "Dare to Whine", "The Roads Not taken, the hidden wisdom in indecision and procrastination."

Look, neither I nor God are trying to demotivate you. It's just that, at the end of the day, all our best efforts are fine. And God wants us to put them forward but compared to the goal of focusing our lives on Christ, they are not that big of a deal.

II. God Can Use our "B" Game More.

One of my favorite Christmas songs, that almost never gets sung, is called, "In the Bleak Midwinter." I guess it never gets sung much because the title isn't that inviting. Bleak! Midwinter! But it is really about this tension of what we bring to Christ. Should we bring our A Game to him, or should we just bring ourselves – our B Game. The lyrics go:

What can I give Him,
Poor as I am? —

If I were a Shepherd
I would bring a lamb;
If I were a Wise Man
I would do my part, —
Yet what I can I give Him, —
Give my heart.

All of us try to bring our best gifts forward. But in the end, it is our hearts, which, let's face it, all get "B's" that God wants. And God can do more with these.

There are a lot of reasons why there is often this chasm between our A Game and our B Game. But one theory is because, really, we put a lot more EGO into our A Game, than our B Game. We put a lot more of ourselves into our A Game than our B Game, but EGO, self is not always what distinguishes greatness. In fact, the less EGO we put into a thing, the better it is. Partly because there is humility, and with humility, there is space for God to insert Godself into what we are doing.

One of the A students who is on staff at Burlpres is Beth Frykberg. And when I told her what I was preaching on this week, she said that she agreed that God could use "B's" more than "A's". She said, "when I have gotten A's I always feel like the work is done, I don't have to do any more work. But when I get B's I know there is work still to be done, and I still have to reach for the A".

III. Christ Lived An "A" Game, So That We Don't Have To.

Jesus was the smartest person ever to live. The best speaker. The best teacher. The greatest ethicist. The greatest healer. The most caring counselor. The most thoughtful friend. There has never been more of an "A Gamer" than Jesus. And yet he died on a cross for us. And why did he die? Because he didn't want us to live with this imbalance of eternal fear within us that says that we have to measure up. Because no one ever can. He didn't want us to be on this rat race for trophies that don't matter. He wanted us to be on the great race for the one thing that does! To reach for it, with all we have got!

CPSIA information can be obtained
at www.ICGtesting.com
Printed in the USA
FSHW022244011218